Planning It	Event management
Concept	Design
Location	Venue
Food	Catering
Fun	Entertainments
Welcome	Hospitality
Creation	Production
Highlights	Details
Get In Touch	Contact

Planning It
Event management

Seamless presentation bears testimony to painstaking hours of preparation.

The perfect host has unlimited time for both their guests' enjoyment and that of their own.

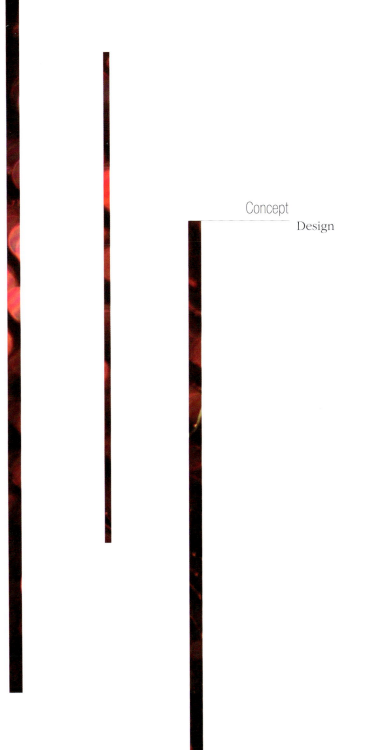

Concept
Design

It is through these working drawings and ideas, that the Best things come to fruition

Without [...] Nothing is and therefo[re] memory has unu[sed]

...why do the been done Before" when the new and origin[al] is the way forward expand the imagination

Enjoy the freedom of design.

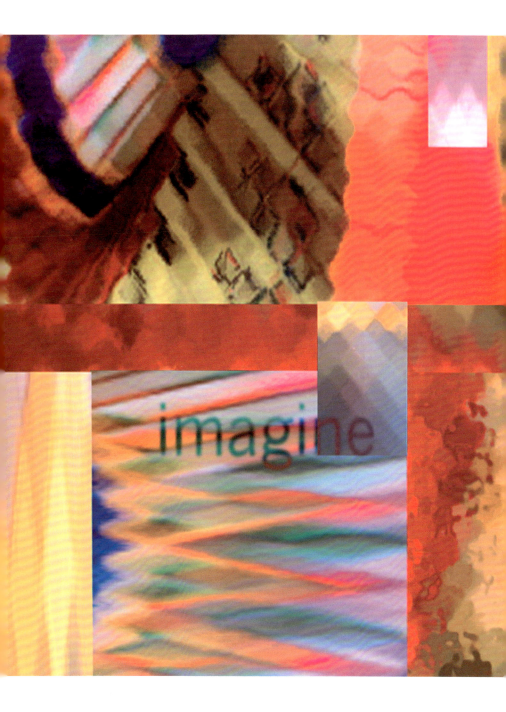

Location Venue

Make a venue out of anywhere...

An enchanted and magical world lies within.

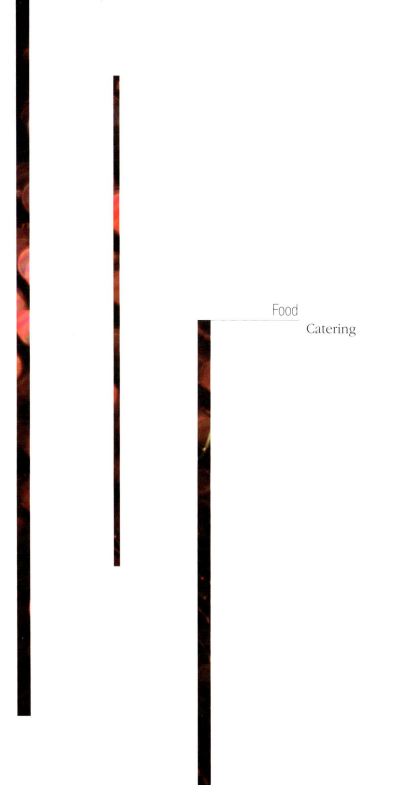

Food
Catering

Ingredients

30 pieces glassware
4 helpings love
72 silver cutlery
3 bags ice
8 passionate kisses
2 quarts olive oil
fine wines
just one wafer thin mint

Method

Gradually mix the ingredients together until a state of perfection is achieved. Blend and season with a pinch of salt. Allow to simmer for approx 10 minutes. Stir vigorously.
Serve hot.

Chin Chin!

You are more important to me than life itself. You bring the nectar to my lips.

Fun
Entertainment

Saturate the senses.

Enjoy performance art
in the extreme.

Even a heavy heart is uplifted
at the sight of smiling faces.

Engines roar.
The crowd cheers.

Welcome
Hospitality

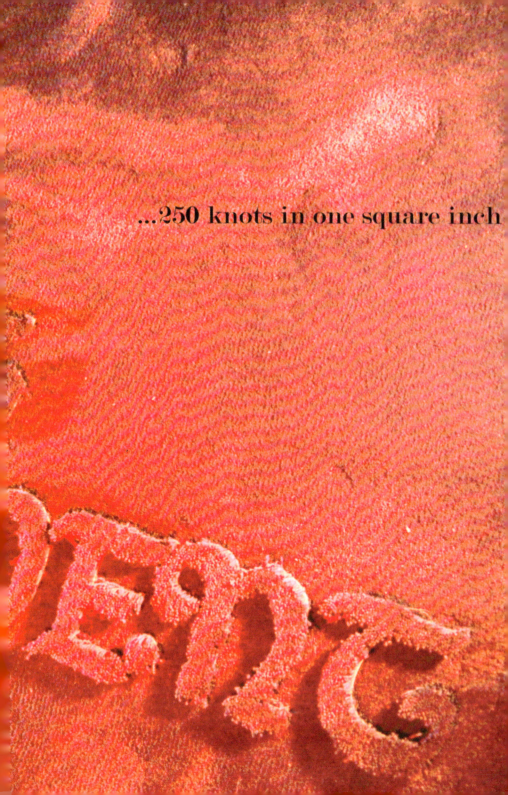

Ladies and gentlemen enjoy luxury commodities in comfortable and air conditioned surroundings.

Creation
Production

the build

Burrow and tunnel deep into the night in the quest
for the sweetest honey.

Highlights
Details

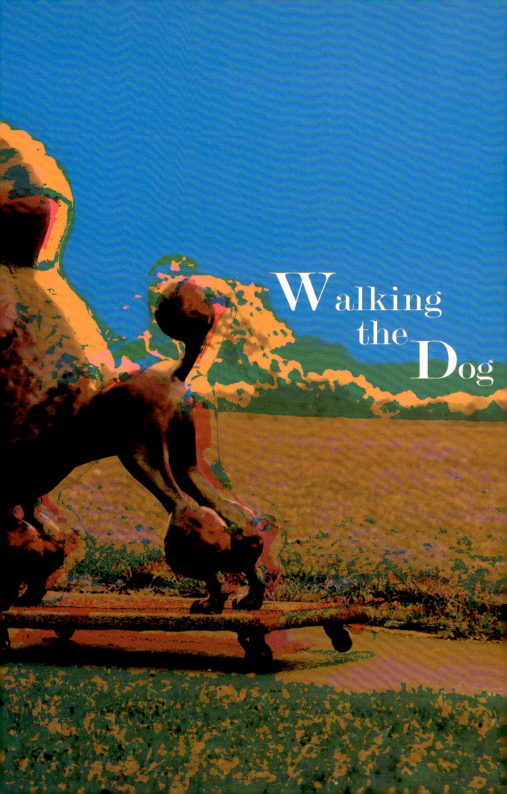

Desire a party planner with full three dimensional experience • Long for water features, fireworks and RSVP service • Relish stage managers, experts, designers and caterers • Indulge in freedom beyond expectation • Enjoy yourself.

Create a lasting memory and enjoy the finishing touches that will put your event head and shoulders above the rest.

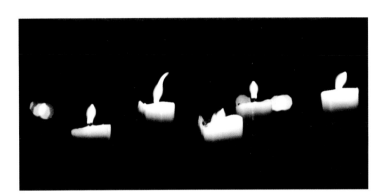

Get In Touch
Contact